VICTOR DOWD AND THE WORLD WAR II GHOST ARMY

Spy on History™

VICTOR DOWD AND THE WORLD WAR II GHOST ARMY

Written by Enigma Alberti
Illustrated by Scott Wegener

WORKMAN PUBLISHING
New York

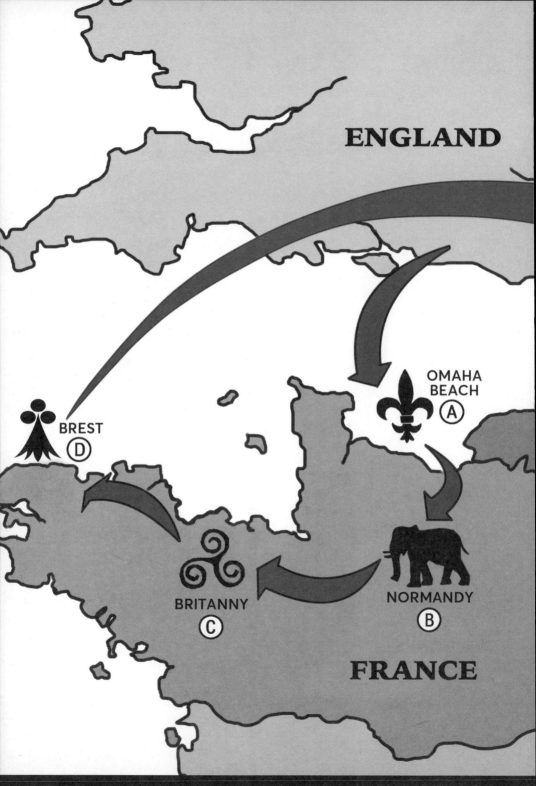

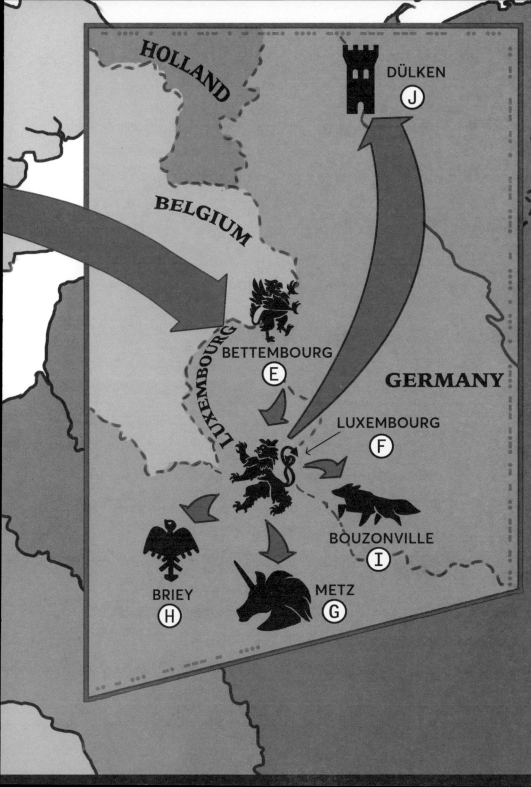

Copyright © 2017 by Workman Publishing Co., Inc.

Text by Enigma Alberti

Illustrations by Scott Wegener

Library of Congress Cataloging-in-Publication Data is available.

ISBN 978-0-7611-9326-5

Designer: Colleen AF Venable and Tae Won Yu
Editor: Daniel Nayeri
Production Editor: Amanda Hong
Production Manager: Julie Primavera

Workman books are available at special discounts when purchased in bulk for premiums and sales promotions as well as for fund-raising or educational use. Special editions or book excerpts can also be created to specification. For details, contact the Special Sales Director at the address below, or send an email to specialmarkets@workman.com.

Workman Publishing Co., Inc.
225 Varick Street
New York, NY 10014-4381
workman.com

WORKMAN is a registered trademark of
Workman Publishing Co., Inc.

SPY ON HISTORY is a trademark of
Workman Publishing Co., Inc.

Printed in China

First printing December 2017

10 9 8 7 6 5 4 3 2 1

This book tells a story full of suspense and intrigue.

But there's also a mystery *in the book itself*.

At the end of the story, you'll find a letter from Victor.

Use the clues in this envelope to decode other clues and codes you'll find throughout the book . . .

to decode the letter and find Victor's hidden sketchbook!

Sergeant Victor Dowd stepped out of the plane onto the metal mesh of the temporary runway.

Just beyond, he could see Omaha Beach.

Last week, it had been the site of the D-Day invasion.

A huge wave of Allied soldiers had crossed the English Channel to France by plane, parachute, and every kind of boat you could imagine.

Their goal:

To take back
France from the
Nazis.

To push those Nazis back into Germany. And to defeat them once and for all.

Those thousands of soldiers had landed on Omaha Beach a week before. But the beach was still full of people.

The sky was still FILLED with planes.

And the ocean was still full of ships, from big carriers to tiny landing craft, as far as the eye could see.

With his first glance around his new surroundings, Vic could also see the casualties. Wounded men lay in rows on the runway, waiting to be airlifted to medical units. Beyond these men, Vic could see the bodies of soldiers who had lost their lives on the beach. They were still waiting to be given a proper burial.

Until this minute, it had been hard for Vic to believe the war was real. He and his fellow platoon members had gone through tough training. They'd learned to march. They'd become experts at using their equipment.

But until today, drills were all they had done.

The night before, Vic had been in the beautiful English countryside, on a date with a nice English girl, far away from the sights and sounds of battle.

He'd known there was a war raging across the channel.

And he'd wanted to get to the front and join the fight.

But even though he had a vivid imagination, he could never have imagined the sights he was seeing now: men milling around on the sand of the beach, tanks and trucks as far as he could see, the wounded lying in rows, the black smudges where shells had exploded.

Or the sounds. Even though the battle on Omaha Beach was over, German machine gun fire still rattled in the distance.

The ferocious German army had turned Europe upside down and threatened the peace and freedom of the whole world.

They were on the defensive after the D-Day invasion, but they were hardly beat.

And some people thought they were the best army in the world.

"Sergeant!" someone called from the plane behind him.

Vic turned around. A bag came flying out of the portal behind him. He caught it just in time. It contained parts for the weapons he and his platoon had been ordered to use against the German army.

They weren't like the other weapons in the other armies in Europe.

Vic's platoon hadn't been issued their own machine guns or heavily armored tanks to protect them.

Instead, they had been ordered to fight the war with guns and tanks and planes made of inflatable rubber.

They'd been specially designed to fool the Germans into thinking there was a large, dangerous force in place, when in fact it was only Vic's platoon and their very big blow-up toys.

The army had assigned just over a thousand men to this secret deception unit—with the code name "Blarney."

But the members of Vic's platoon, the Fourth Platoon of Company D, led by Lieutenant Bernie

Mason, comprised the first fifteen men out of all of them to arrive in France.

Before they brought the rest of the deception unit over, the army wanted to see if this crazy idea of using blow-up tanks to fool the Germans would really work.

Vic's platoon's mission: to protect the first heavy-artillery battalion to land in France after D-Day. To do that, they were supposed to set up dummy guns a mile ahead of the artillery's actual line.

The object: to draw German fire away from the real artillery and toward the fake.

In other words, Vic and his platoon would know their deception had worked if the Germans started shelling them.

((•–ᴡᴡᴡᴡᴡᴡᴠ (((•))) ᴡᴡᴡᴡᴡᴡᴡ•)))

The officers who dreamed up this secret deception unit called it the Twenty-Third Headquarters Special Troops.

The men who were in it called it the

Ghost Army.

It was a top secret project—so top secret that nobody really told enlisted men like Vic everything that was really going on.

But during the few months before D-Day, when many

of the members of the Ghost Army had trained together at an English country estate called Walton Hall, they'd had some time to figure it out.

Vic was part of the 603rd Engineer Camouflage Battalion Special. This was the largest division in the Ghost Army, with close to four hundred men.

Before they arrived in England, they'd spent the past two years doing camouflage work. They'd helped develop and test the inflatable guns, planes, tanks, and vehicles that Vic's company was about to try out for the first time against the Germans. Some of Vic's unit had even camouflaged important military sites in the United States. They'd used their artistic talents to disguise bomber planes and coastal defenses so that it looked as if nothing was there if spy planes looked down at them from the sky.

Most of the men of the 603rd hadn't been recruited through the normal draft. They'd been handpicked for their skills in drawing and design from art schools all over the country, but especially from Philly and New York.

Vic, who was from Brooklyn, had gone to Pratt, a New York art school. He'd only been out for a few years and was working at a comics studio, drawing characters like Bulletman, Captain Midnight, and Spy Smasher, when the dean of his art school asked if Vic would consider joining a special unit of army artists.

At Walton Hall, their leaders had told all the men that the Twenty-Third Headquarters Special Troops would be a kind of traveling show, putting on a performance for a very tough audience: the German army.

Vic's unit, the 603rd, would set the stage with their inflatables and other camouflage work.

But the show played on that stage would be presented by two other groups: the signal company and the sonic unit.

The men of the Signal Company Special were top-notch radio operators.

It was their job to imitate the radio transmissions of whatever unit the Ghost Army was ordered to impersonate.

Why?

So that the Germans who were listening in would believe there was a unit where the Ghost Army had set up camp. Then the real unit could move somewhere else, without the Germans knowing where they'd gone.

One of the things Allied forces had learned early in the war was that German spies were great at picking up Allied radio transmissions. Just by listening in on radio traffic, the Germans could guess, very accurately, where Allied troops were and what they were doing.

The GERMANS

listened

so closely to Allied radio transmissions that they could tell one unit from another by their radio habits. The Germans knew how often different units sent messages.

They knew what kinds of messages each unit sent. They knew the names and nicknames of men in different units.

The Germans could even tell different Morse code operators apart, because every person tapped out code a little differently—the same way every person has different handwriting.

So if the radio operators in the Ghost Army wanted to convince the Germans of the existence of a phantom unit, they were going to need to copy that unit's radio habits perfectly.

And getting it right could be a matter of life or death, not just for the men of the Ghost Army but for the soldiers in other companies whose lives they were assigned to protect.

To do all this, the signal company learned everything they could about the radio habits of the unit they had to imitate. They were so good at this that they could even mimic the different ways each radio operator tapped out Morse code.

The men of the sonic company were the other players in the Ghost Army's show. Officially known as the 3132 Signal Service Company Special, their job was sound effects.

They'd spent the past months making recordings of trucks and men moving in, bridges being built, and orders being given—any sounds that would fool the enemy into thinking there was a big force somewhere even when there wasn't.

The sonic company had created an entire library of sounds, including tanks moving around, trucks starting up, and officers shouting. They kept them on miles of magnetized wire, because wire wouldn't skip when it played back like a record did.

Depending on the illusion they wanted to create, the sonic company would mix programs of different sounds from their library together. Then they would play them

from giant speakers mounted on the backs of half-tracks: vehicles with wheels on the front and tank tracks on the back. The half-tracks were specially designed so that the speakers could fold into them and completely disappear. When one was on the move, it looked like just another regular piece of army equipment.

Most of the men in the sonic company had experience working with sound. But the sonic company also had several weathermen in the unit. Temperature and wind have a big effect on how sound travels. So they always had to take the weather into account.

One other unit was part of the Ghost Army, too. The 406th Engineer Combat Company Special included the only trained fighting soldiers in the group—not quite two hundred men out of the thousand total.

The combat engineers provided security to keep snoopers away from Ghost Army deceptions. The last thing the Ghost Army wanted was to have a local civilian wander into one of their camps and realize they were armed with nothing more than a bunch of rubber tanks.

But the combat company also helped create the deceptions. They dug real tank and artillery positions for the phony dummies. And they set up real explosives to create flashes that made it look like the rubber guns could really fire.

All the men of the Ghost Army were handpicked and highly skilled.

But almost none of them had been trained for combat.

The combat engineers had. But there were only enough of them to defend the unit, not to attack.

And almost no one in the Ghost Army had ever seen any action.

So in the Ghost Army, soldiers like Vic were in a very strange position.

It was their job to get the Germans to shoot at them.

But they weren't equipped to shoot back.

((•‿‿‿‿‿‿‿‿‿‿‿‿‿((•))‿‿‿‿‿‿‿‿‿‿•))

Vic and his platoon spent their first night in France in a foxhole with German artillery fire raining down all around them.

"I don't know how you did it," one of his buddies told Vic when he woke up the next morning. "You were the only one of us who got any sleep."

Before the platoon left Omaha Beach, Vic had time to make a quick sketch: a German "potato masher" hand grenade left lying on the ground next to an empty helmet.

From then on, there wasn't much time to draw.

Vic and his platoon had brought their inflatable dummies over to France with them. But the dummies were huge and heavy. And apparently nobody had thought to arrange any transport for them once they got to France.

So the first order of business was to scrounge transport for them and their gear.

Once they found a truck, they caught up with the artillery group they were assigned to impersonate, which had already moved inland from the beach.

Then Vic and the rest of his platoon swung into action.

About a mile from the real artillery line, they dug in positions for their inflatable howitzers. They covered the fake guns with real camo netting so the guns looked camouflaged—but still visible to enemy aircraft.

The combat company improvised flash canisters that went off when the real guns fired, to make it look like the shells came from the inflatables.

And then they all waited.

It was hard to believe that they could get the Germans to waste real shells firing on a bunch of rubber guns.

And it was a strange feeling to *hope* that the Germans would fire on them.

But then the first shell landed. And then another.

It was clear the Germans were aiming for them, and not for the soldiers behind them with real guns—the real artillery line.

That month, Vic's platoon moved into ten different sites with the artillery unit they were assigned to protect as they moved up the French peninsula.

Again and again,

landed GERMAN shells around the dummy guns of the

GHOST ARMY—

and not the real guns farther back.

Again and again, Vic and his buddies scrambled for cover as the shells fell around them.

Despite all those shells, the Ghost Army platoon made it through their first operation with no casualties.

It wasn't fun to be fired on, especially when they had no guns to shoot back.

But they had still won a victory.

There was no question their first deception had fooled the Germans.

The crazy idea of using blow-up tanks and guns to trick the enemy had worked.

Most of the Ghost Army caught up with Vic's platoon in late June.

The sonic company was still over in England, putting the final touches on their sonic spoofs.

But when Vic and his platoon were released from their work with the artillery unit, they met up with the rest of their camouflage unit. They were camped in fields outside a small French town. And the signal company was with them, too.

For several days, the camouflage company tested the new equipment they'd brought with them from England. They set up every single dummy to make sure they all still worked.

One of those days, two Frenchmen on bikes somehow managed to get through their top secret security perimeter.

The first thing they saw was four American GIs picking

up a forty-ton Sherman tank.

The bicyclists watched in shock, wondering how in the world four men could lift something so heavy.

"The Americans are very strong," someone told them as they were hustled away.

((•~wwwwwwwwww~www ((•)) ~www~wwwwwwwww~•))

Now that most of the Ghost Army was assembled in France, it wasn't long before they got their first assignment.

The mission of Operation Elephant was simple.

The Second Armored Division was moving up to the fighting line.

But they wanted to keep that news secret from the Germans for as long as possible.

So the Ghost Army was assigned to make it seem like the armored division was still in place, far from the battle, even after they had started to move up for the fight.

The plan: As the unit moved out, the Ghost Army would replace them with dummies,

setting up a
fake tank
or inflatable gun in the place of each real one.

From the beginning, the operation was a mess.

For one thing, orders weren't well coordinated at the top.

So the real Second Armored moved out in broad daylight instead of under cover of night. And they moved on the main roads where anybody could see them.

If a German informant spotted the real Second Armored on the move, then the whole Ghost Army deception would be for nothing.

Not only that, it might get the Germans wondering why another unit was pretending to be the Second Armored. They might even realize that the Allies were using a top secret deception unit.

But despite the mistakes at the top,

the Ghost Army didn't give up.

They spent the next two days setting up a hundred inflatables and camouflage nets—and a dummy airstrip.

But they had a lot to learn themselves.

It was amazing how much they hadn't thought of.

Sometime during the operation, someone realized that real tanks make tracks—unlike inflatable dummies. A tank that didn't make tracks was a dead giveaway as a fake.

So the Ghost Army combat unit started using their bulldozers to make tracks for the fake tanks.

"You know," someone realized, "the same thing is true for our inflatable guns. If we were really using them, there'd be artillery shells all over the place."

So the Ghost Army started piling spent artillery shells around their fake guns.

"And a lot of soldiers usually make a big mess," someone else recognized. "They build a lot of fires. They hang out a lot of laundry."

So the Ghost Army started building fires and hanging out laundry—and spending as much time as possible outside so that it looked like there were even more men stationed inside, unseen.

In Vic's camouflage unit, the conversation was all about how to make their camouflage convincing.

"A real unit would never park a tank without covering it with camouflage netting," they reasoned.

So Vic's company had to use camouflage nets, too, to look like a real unit.

But it turned out that Vic's camouflage group was a bit *too* good at camouflage.

They did such a good job of camouflaging their inflatable tanks and trucks that some of them were completely hidden.

Friendly Allied pilots flew over the spot and couldn't see anything there.

But the whole goal of the camouflage unit was for the Germans to catch sight of their fake equipment.

So Vic's company learned to thin out their camo mesh. Sitting around in the camp, they pulled half of the fabric strips out of every net so that the tanks and guns below would be visible.

To do this job, the camouflage experts had to get worse at camouflage.

Nobody was sure if the Ghost Army's first big deception had worked or not.

But they knew for certain that they had learned a lot.

The biggest lesson: They couldn't always follow the plans they'd been given. Because once they got close to the front line, things were always changing.

For one thing, the German air force, known as the Luftwaffe, was losing strength. They weren't flying nearly as many flights as they had earlier in the war.

So Vic's camouflage company realized they wouldn't be putting on their show for planes in the sky. They'd need to fool people on the ground.

That wouldn't just involve dummies and camouflage nets. It would mean putting on a show that could convince anybody who came by that they were traveling with

far more men,

and far more

FIREPOWER,

than they actually had.

So Vic's company started to develop "poop sheets" for every US division.

A poop sheet collected all the information they could get on a unit so that it could be used to create a convincing imitation. Vic's company collected every detail they could get: the code names a unit used, the markings they put on their vehicles, how their signs were painted—even how their uniforms were worn.

Whenever the Ghost Army planned a deception in the future, they vowed, everyone would be briefed about the unit they were impersonating. They'd know that unit's history and be able to talk about that unit's officers—just as if they were in it.

But no matter how much new work they took on, the men of the Ghost Army still found a little time to make art.

Not even the war could stop them.

No matter where they were, they still drew and sketched and painted.

Sometimes they used nothing more than ink and spit. And they worked on everything from notebooks to old receipts.

They drew each other. They drew families who had been displaced by the war. They traveled to a bombed-out church in a nearby town, where the town's children collected pieces of broken stained glass and asked to trade it with the soldiers for their chocolate.

It was hard to see the destruction the German army had left behind in France.

But it also helped Vic and his buddies know what they were fighting for.

When their next order came,

they'd be ready.

((•⁃⅃⅃⅃⅃⅃⅃⅃⅃⅃⅃⁃⅃⅃⅃⁃((•))⁃⅃⅃⅃⁃⅃⅃⅃⅃⅃⅃⅃⅃⅃⁃•))

In late July, seven weeks after the D-Day landing that had brought Vic to France, the Allies finally broke through German defenses.

General George Patton's Third Army was poised to sweep across France in a race to surround the German army—and defeat it.

But to do that, Patton wanted the element of surprise.

So the Ghost Army was called into action.

Their mission: to make it look as if the Allies planned to head *west*, not east.

If the Ghost Army succeeded, the Germans would defend the wrong place.

And that meant the Germans would have less to throw at Patton when he really did strike.

In early August, the Ghost Army went to work.

They broke into four separate groups, each portraying a real division.

But they all had one thing in common: All four of them headed west to confuse the German generals.

For days, the men of the signal company kept up a steady stream of fake radio messages in hopes the Germans would intercept them and believe they were real units moving in.

Vic's division set up more than seventy inflatable tanks.

And they did everything else they could think of to make the Germans believe that there was a real military unit in the area.

They stenciled the bumpers of their trucks and jeeps with the markings of the division they were impersonating. They wandered around nearby towns wearing that division's patches.

If they couldn't get patches, no problem. There were so many artists in their ranks that someone would just paint a patch right onto a jacket.

Two members of the Ghost Army even got the bright idea to dress up like American military police. To give the impression that there was a real division in town, they went into a dozen bars. They'd walk in and announce to everyone that the Americans were heading out, so any GIs in the bar better get going.

By the end of the operation, the men had started to refer to all this set making and playacting as "special effects."

It felt like putting on a play.

But they were playing on a deadly stage.

As usual, the Ghost Army knew they'd done their job when they got fired on.

They could tell that German fire increased after they put on a "show."

But they had another way to

31

tell that the Germans were "listening in" on their radio transmissions. The Germans had special transmitters designed to jam the radio signals and spoil the communications of nearby Allied troops. And they were using them to jam Ghost Army radios.

That meant the Germans were hearing their radio deceptions—and responding to them.

It was a strange kind of applause to get.

But what mattered most to the Ghost Army was that the Germans stayed just where the Allies wanted them to—long enough for Patton to surround them.

When the last Germans on the French coast realized they'd been defeated, they retreated in a panic.

Along the way, they abandoned all kinds of equipment.

Fifty thousand of them were captured.

The rest were on the run.

The Allies broke out of Normandy at last and began to

sweep across

FRANCE,

and the Ghost Army went with them.

By the end of August, only a handful of Germans were left in France.

The ones who held the port of Brest, at the tip of the Brittany peninsula, though, were tough.

They'd been under siege for weeks, but they showed no signs of giving up.

So the Ghost Army was called in.

Their job this time: to impersonate an armored division so that the German general Ramcke would think he was facing more tanks than the Americans actually had.

If the plan worked, the Germans would move their antitank weapons and soldiers to their flanks to defend themselves against the Ghost Army's inflatable tanks.

That way, it would be easier for the Allies to attack the Germans in Brest.

The Ghost Army's sonic company had finally arrived from England with their wire recordings of troops marching, generals shouting, trucks moving, and bridges being built.

This was the first time the Ghost Army would get to use all their deception tactics at once: visual, radio, and sonic.

But the weather didn't cooperate.

Vic and his company traveled two days through the rain to get to Brest.

And when they arrived: more rain.

But that didn't stop the sonic company from putting on their first show of the whole war.

As soon as they arrived, they drove their trucks right up to the German front line.

And when night fell, just five hundred yards away from the German guns, the sonic company set the stage.

It was an eerie experience for Vic and his buddies to hear the disembodied sounds rolling through the darkness.

The sonic unit started by playing the sound of one tank approaching. Then the sound of another tank. Then, layering recording on top of recording, they played the sounds of a whole convoy of

tanks
and
heavy
trucks moving **in.**

They played the sounds of recorded bushes crackling.

They played the sounds of recorded gears shifting.

"No, no, no!" recorded voices called through the night. "Not here. Over there. That's right."

The sound was so realistic that it was hard for Vic to believe it wasn't real.

Through it all was the sound of the rain.

It was all too real: cold and steady.

As the rain poured down on them, Vic's company set up their dummy tanks, jeeps, and trucks.

"Hurry up," one soldier told another. "We've got a hundred of these to set up by morning."

"This one's done."

"You call that done? It's not even half-inflated."

"Are you kidding me? It was full a minute ago."

"These valves leak in the rain," someone else called over to them. "Just to make life more interesting."

"You're right," the first soldier said. "The gun on this tank is drooping all the way to the ground."

"We've got to get it right by morning. That's a dead giveaway."

((•-ⱲⱲⱲⱲⱲⱲⱲⱲⱲⱲ-ⱲⱲ- ((•)) -ⱲⱲ-ⱲⱲⱲⱲⱲⱲⱲⱲ-•))

Soaked and tired, Vic's group was still up at first light to begin the "special effects."

They lit fires, pitched tents, and hung laundry—all to make it look like there were ten times more of them than there really were.

They switched the patches on their jackets.

They painted new markings on their trucks.

They drove the trucks back and forth to town.

That night, they got their first sign that the deception was working—when the Germans started to shell their phony position.

The Germans had moved dozens of antitank guns away from the actual fighting. They were using them now to shoot at a Ghost Army armed with nothing but sound and special effects.

So Vic and his company dug real shelters in the ground to protect themselves from the German artillery barrage.

But every shell that fell around them was a small victory. The surrounded Germans were almost out of ammunition. That meant that every shot they made brought them closer to defeat.

And every shell they sent toward the Ghost Army's position was a shell that wouldn't land somewhere else to harm another Allied soldier.

$$((\bullet\text{-}\wedge\wedge\wedge\wedge\wedge\wedge\wedge\wedge\wedge\text{-}((\bullet)))\text{-}\wedge\wedge\wedge\wedge\wedge\wedge\wedge\wedge\text{-}\bullet))$$

As the Ghost Army held down their position outside Brest, the Allies liberated Paris.

The German general who held Brest was tough. The Allies had hoped to force him to surrender early, but he held out for a month longer.

By that time, the Ghost Army had been ordered to new quarters in Saint-Germain, just twenty miles outside Paris.

The Parisians were still celebrating.

And the mood in Vic's company was triumphant.

Sure, the Germans were still giving Patton a hard time in some places.

But

PARIS was free.

It was hard to believe the Germans could fight much longer. A lot of men in the Ghost Army figured the war might be over in a month.

None of them could wait to get home.

But in the meantime, they had Paris.

(((•-ᴡᴡᴡᴡᴡᴡᴡᴡᴡᴡᴡᴡᴡ-ᴡᴡᴡ-(((•)))-ᴡᴡᴡ-ᴡᴡᴡᴡᴡᴡᴡᴡᴡᴡᴡ-•)))

Paris wasn't just the capital of France. Many people thought it was the world capital of art. It was full of architecture, fashion, museums—and girls.

So the men of the Ghost Army went into Paris every chance they got.

Vic hitched his first ride into Paris in a sidecar attached to the motorcycle of an eccentric Englishman who had settled in Saint-Germain after the Great War, twenty years before.

Vic had seen pictures of the great avenue of the Champs-Elysées and the giant arch of the Arc de Triomphe. But when he caught sight of them, growing closer and closer as he approached the city, it was hard to believe he was seeing them with his own eyes.

Those days after Paris was liberated were something special.

And so were the Paris girls. They wore bright clothes and had incredible hairdos. And there was nothing they found more interesting than a man in uniform.

Some of his buddies flipped frantically through their French-English dictionaries, trying to find just the right phrase to impress the French girls.

Others walked the streets alone, wrestling with everything they'd seen during the war.

It was easy to get to know the Parisians. Everyone was eager for the cigarettes, chocolate, and cheese that American soldiers had with them.

As soon as Vic got there, he started sketching everything he saw: girls on bikes, people in bars.

It was a relief to use his talent just to make a quick picture—instead of using it to fool the Germans and bring enemy fire down on his own head.

But those first magical days after the liberation of Paris couldn't last forever.

The war, it turned out, wasn't really over yet.

Not by a

long shot.

Ceneral Patton and his army swept across France at an incredible pace, driving out the Germans as they went.

In fact, at least one Ghost Army operation was canceled because Patton was moving so fast that no one could catch up with him.

But a few weeks after the liberation of Paris, Patton stopped to mass his troops for a new attack.

His goal this time: to dislodge the Germans from the French fortified city of Metz.

But there was a

problem.

Patton had moved so quickly across France that a

had opened in his line.

North of Metz, for an entire seventy miles, there were no Allied forces. Just one single group of cavalry.

That single cavalry group would be no match for the German forces that faced Patton and his army if the Germans got wise to the gap.

And if the Germans stormed through that gap, they could easily surround Patton—and smash the Allied forces.

If that happened, there was no telling how much longer the war would drag on—or who would win.

So until another real division could fill that seventy-mile gap, the Ghost Army was called in.

They'd drawn German attention away from the real fighting in Brittany.

They'd fooled the German general under siege at Brest.

But until now, they'd always been in the background, supporting real troops.

They'd never been called on to do anything like this: Impersonate an entire division at the most dangerous point in the great showdown between the Allies and the Nazis.

And this time, they wouldn't just be protecting the lives of one other division.

The fate of Patton's whole army—and the course of the whole war—hung in the balance.

To the relief of Vic and his company, the plan only called for two and a half days of deception before a real unit would move in to relieve them.

That short time frame was key.

This time they'd be playing their "show" right on the front lines. And they knew from experience that Germans were excellent at discovering the identity of Allied units when they moved up to the front.

So once they joined the line themselves, all eyes would be on them.

Every shoulder patch, every camouflage net, every phony salute and radio broadcast, would be under intense scrutiny.

 **The** tiniest mistake could **alert** the **Germans** to the fact that the **Ghost Army was**n't who they pretended to be.

That would blow their cover as a deception unit, so the Germans would be on guard against any future deceptions for the rest of the war.

Even worse, it could also prove deadly for the Ghost Army. Their radios and loudspeakers and camouflage weren't much defense against an invading German army.

And if the German army was provoked to roll over the Ghost Army, the entire Allied force would be at risk.

It wasn't an easy position to take.

But it was only for two and a half days.

They could fool the Germans that long, the men in Vic's company told themselves.

Just long enough for the real fighting division to arrive.

The Ghost Army pulled into Bettembourg, Luxembourg, just south of Luxembourg City, after two hundred and fifty miles of hard travel from their camp outside Paris.

Their mission was simple: to join the front line.

But that was made harder by the fact that the gap in Patton's line was so big nobody knew quite where the front line *was*.

Before the Ghost Army could even move into position, they had to go find the Germans.

And when their scouts located the German lines, the Germans were a lot closer than anyone would have liked— only about two miles from the Ghost Army's current position.

But nothing was going to stop the Ghost Army from doing what they came to do.

At three in the morning, the deception began.

First the sonic team went to work.

Vic heard the sounds of vehicles cutting tracks through the forest, loudspeakers blaring, sergeants' voices yelling: "Put out that cigarette! Now!"

Even though he knew it was all a show, it sure sounded like a whole division was moving in. In fact, the sounds were so real that some men actually began to see tanks in the dark. But Vic knew all too well that they weren't a whole division and they didn't have a single real tank to fight with.

They were only a handful of men with a few good tricks.

Did they have what it takes to fool the Germans and hold the line?

Before first light the next morning, Vic was up again, sewing needle in hand. Someone had come through the day before, handing out patches for the Sixth Armored Division—the unit the Ghost Army was impersonating.

Vic sewed his patch to the shoulder of his uniform, which was starting to look a little ragged from switching out so many patches.

Then he went out to greet the day.

He wasn't working on much sleep, and neither was anyone else.

He and his company had been up for most of the previous night. They'd wrestled their inflatables into place in the dark and set the stage with spent shells and camo nets.

Now, as light dawned, men roved among the inflatables, putting on the finishing touches.

One pair of men scrambled to reinflate a tank with a drooping gun.

"Who camouflaged this truck?" an officer bellowed, yanking at the netting to reveal the shine of the front window. "You couldn't see it at all!"

As soon as the sun came up, THE SHOW BEGAN.

All day, the Ghost Army put on a tense play, doing everything they could to imitate an actual infantry battalion.

They collected firewood and congregated around the fires.

They did laundry and hung it out.

"My mom would be so proud of me," one soldier joked. "I've washed this shirt twice since the last time I wore it."

"You actually washed yours?" his buddy said. "I just threw mine in the river and took it back out."

They posted signs along the main supply routes.

They set up military checkpoints, just like a real division would do, to control who came in and out of their area.

And they set up a water point outside town, because no big group of men could survive for long without a lot of water. If it didn't seem like they were using enough, the locals might get suspicious about what was going on.

And they painted Sixth Armored Division markings on their trucks.

"Finally, they let us paint," one soldier said with satisfaction, admiring his work as a truck rolled in, just returned from town.

"Don't get too attached to your masterpiece," his buddy said, slapping a swath of army green paint over the neat stencil lettering they'd applied just hours before.

"Hey, what's the big idea?" his friend asked.

"We're putting new markings on it," his buddy said, "and sending it back to town so they think it's a whole different truck."

Everyone in the Ghost Army had been briefed on the history of the Sixth Armored. And the men who were sent to town in the trucks had been told to use it.

They went into every bar and café in town and made sure everyone they talked to knew what unit they were with.

"There's no unit like the Sixth Armored," they'd proclaim over a beer.

"I've been over here with the Sixth Armored for a year," they'd tell the waitress.

"This is nothing," they'd tell a worried housewife on the street. "We're not even all here yet. Wait till tomorrow. There are three times more of us moving in tonight."

In the meantime, the radio corps brought in all their transmitters, headsets, and codebooks. They set up three phony radio networks, faking the radio traffic of the Sixth Armored, down to the unique patterns of their telegraph operators.

Just across the Moselle River, the Germans watched and listened.

So did the local civilians.
  That day, the Ghost Army had seen people taking notes as they rolled past. Some had even photographed the Ghost Army vehicles.

But attention meant DANGER.

If even one civilian got the idea that their tanks were dummies, the whole game was over.

"Pack them away," Vic's unit was told. "They think the inflatables are too risky for this one."

From now on, the deception would go on with just sound and special effects.

A few real tanks arrived that evening.

And Vic and his company spent the whole night taking the inflatables down.

As they did, the sonic unit broadcast the arrival of even more men, trucks, and tanks.

The next morning, they kept up their deception in town.

Since they were pretending more men had arrived overnight, they drew even more water from the water point near Bettembourg.

It was Sunday, so some men went to church in town, making sure no one could miss that they were with the Sixth Armored.

That afternoon, Ghost Army observers watching the German front line saw new units moving into place.

"You see that?" one said. "They're moving men into place to meet us. They think we're a threat. They think we're the real Sixth Armored."

"I'd feel more celebratory if that didn't mean we've now got even more German guns aimed at us," his buddy said.

But at least the deception was almost over.

All they had to do was hang on until the next day, when the real division would move into place and the Ghost Army would fade away.

EXCEPT the
real division didn't come.

The Eighty-Third Infantry Division had been assigned to take the place of the Ghost Army to fill the hole in Patton's line.

But they had been delayed.

In their place came two assault gun troops and a tank company.

But they were hardly a match for the huge numbers of Germans across the river.

And those Germans were getting aggressive.

The next day, telephone wires laid by the radio company were found cut.

Shots were fired on men collecting water at the water point.

Ghost Army outposts reported Germans in the woods just outside camp.

The Ghost Army's small force of combat engineers mounted machine guns on their trucks and started to patrol the roads between the front lines, sometimes in full view of the Germans.

Vic and the other men in his company did everything they could think of to keep up the deception that they were members of an entire artillery division with thousands of men.

The radio operators kept up their phony transmissions. They checked in with headquarters. They reported on the movements of German troops. They cracked the same kinds of corny jokes the Sixth Armored radio operators were known to crack from time to time.

The sonic units broadcast sounds of bridge building and troop movement for four nights straight.

Vic knew that every moment the deception stretched on, the chances that they'd be discovered only grew.

But he also knew they were the only Allied soldiers who stood between Patton and the hostile German army.

Finally, seven days after the Ghost Army took up their position in Patton's line, the Eighty-Third Infantry arrived.

The deception had lasted almost three times as long as planned.

German patrols had increased in the area after the Ghost Army arrived—which also increased the chance that the Germans would see through their deception.

While the Ghost Army held the line, the Germans had moved in two whole infantry divisions across the river.

That took some pressure off American troops in the south.

But most important, the Ghost Army had kept the whole German army from recognizing that they stood just across the river from a gap of seventy unprotected miles.

With not much more than radios, paint, and imagination, the Ghost Army had held the Allied line.

As Vic and his company drove into Luxembourg City at the end of September, the streets were lined with cheering crowds waving American flags.

The city had just been liberated, and its people were ready to celebrate.

His camouflage company was given an old seminary as barracks.

The Germans who had been there before had taken out all the furniture, but that wasn't what bothered the artists of the Ghost Army the most. What really drove them nuts was the terrible art the Germans had left behind: Nazi murals painted all over the walls.

Free Luxembourg City gave the men a warm welcome. The town hadn't been destroyed by the war. The people were friendly. And Vic wasn't the only man in the division who was glad to discover they even had art supply stores.

But the Ghost Army's deception work was far from over.

All that fall, using Luxembourg City as a base, they put on show after show.

The Allied army was at a standstill on the German border for all of October, planning their next assault. But when the Allies went on the move again in November, the Ghost Army was at the heart of the action.

Heavy artillery guns were often the first clue the enemy got about where an army planned to attack. Before big guns could be used, they had to be hauled into place.

That gave enemy generals a very good idea of where an attack might come from. And if they knew that, they had a chance to prepare their defenses.

Unless they were fooled by the phony artillery of the Ghost Army.

On the cutting edge of the new Allied offensive, the Ghost Army worked overtime, creating fake artillery units so that the real ones could move into place and launch surprise attacks.

But that wasn't the Ghost Army's only trick. They also covered the infantry movements. They broadcast radio and sound and created special effects to make it seem as if infantry divisions were retreating to rest—when in fact they were moving up into the front lines.

This close to the front lines, Vic and his company were always under fire.

They dug their foxholes deep.

But **nobody** ever knew where the next **SHELL** would fall or **who** might get **HIT.**

((•·ᴡᴡᴡᴡᴡᴡᴡᴡᴡᴠᴠᴡᴡ ((•)) ᴡᴡᴡᴡᴡᴡᴡᴡᴡ•))

For Thanksgiving, the men got an early Christmas present.

The movie star Marlene Dietrich arrived to sing for them. Lieutenant Bernie Mason, who led Vic's platoon, was the lucky guy who got to introduce her to the audience.

They even had real turkey for dinner.

But in Luxembourg City, the mood was growing tense.

Shots rang out every night.

The city was still full of people who were loyal to the Germans.

No one was sure who to trust.

Up at the German line, the Allies had launched an all-out attack, fighting a bloody advance through the Hürtgen Forest.

But south of the main battle, a thin spot had opened in the line.

When they'd held the line for Patton, nobody had been sure if the deception would work.

But by now, the Ghost Army were old hands at this.

They swung into action just north of Luxembourg City, imitating the Seventy-Fifth Infantry Division with every trick in their book.

They ran fake convoys up near the front line.

They broadcast the sounds of troop movements.

They set up radio networks.

They created a water point.

They posted military police checkpoints.

Harry Reeder, the commander of the whole Ghost Army, even put on fake general's stars and made a phony visit to their phony command center.

But this time it was the Ghost Army's turn to be surprised.

It turned out that the Allied commanders weren't the

only ones who had noticed that the area was thinly held.

Hitler had seen the opportunity, too.

The Ghost Army had been trying to attract German forces to the area.

But more German forces than they had ever dreamed of were moving in.

Hitler had amassed a huge force to launch his own surprise attack through the Ardennes.

Exactly where the Ghost Army had been stationed for the past week.

The Ghost Army now stood directly in Hitler's path.

As shells began to fall through the trees and gunfire rang through the woods, the Ghost Army fell back.

With the Battle of the Bulge raging behind them, they returned to their quarters in Luxembourg City.

There they prepared for a full-scale retreat.

Vic and his division were given orders to set explosive charges on the vehicles that carried their equipment and inflatables. Even if they had to destroy their tools, they never wanted the Germans to learn their deception secrets.

As German planes flew over, strafing the city below, men from the Ghost Army scrambled up to the roof of the seminary, where they set up a machine gun nest.

All night long, members of the Ghost Army took turns shooting back at the Germans overhead.

It was the first and last time any of them would get a

chance to take an actual shot at the enemy.

After all the time they'd spent under enemy fire with no way to fight back, it felt good to take a shot.

But no matter how much fight the Allies put up, either on that seminary roof or on the front lines, Hitler's surprise attack was too strong to match.

A few days later, nobody could deny that the Allied lines

had broken.

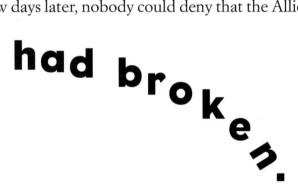

In the Ardennes forest, Allied forces were in chaos.

As the front line collapsed, most of the American troops headed west toward Luxembourg City.

Suddenly the streets were flooded with retreating troops.

To make room for them, the Ghost Army was ordered to fall back.

Leaving Luxembourg, their home base for months, was tough.

Heavy December snow poured down as the Ghost Army moved out.

Vic watched as Luxembourgers replaced the American flags in their windows with white flags of surrender. Or even Nazi swastikas.

Just weeks before, he and the other men had thought the war was almost over.

Now nobody knew when the fighting would ever stop. Or who would be the victor when it did.

Less than a week later, it was Christmas.

Vic couldn't help thinking back to Christmases when he was a kid in Brooklyn.

In New York, the streets were hung with lights. Men sold Christmas trees from the sidewalk while crowds of happy shoppers walked by. And if Vic could get a nickel from his mom or dad, he could buy himself a bag of roasted chestnuts from a holiday stand.

This Christmas could hardly be more different from that.

The Ghost Army was stationed in Verdun, in cold, wet, dirty barracks from World War I.

Verdun, as everyone in the Ghost Army knew, was one of the great battlefields of the First World War.

Twenty-eight years earlier, almost half a million soldiers, just like them, had lost their lives there.

In the window of one of the barracks, a skull lay unburied, helmet still on.

It wasn't exactly a cheerful Christmas decoration.

And this winter was the coldest one France had seen in forty years.

Still, Vic and his company tried to celebrate.

The Ghost Army decorated a Christmas tree with garlands of paper and stars cut from tin cans. And they threw a party for the refugee children who were also taking shelter at Verdun.

As tough as the men had it, they knew these children had it tougher.

The men of the Ghost Army still had their own families, safe back in the United States.

But many of these children had lost both their mothers and their fathers.

So the men of the Ghost Army made up dozens of boxes for the children and filled them with goodies from their own rations: candy, gum, and other food.

As he passed the presents out, Vic couldn't help noticing a little boy with incredibly sad eyes. The boy had opened his box to see the treats hidden inside. But no matter what anybody did, they couldn't get him to smile.

God knows what he's been through, Vic thought.

But if the Allies couldn't turn the tide of the war, Vic knew, all of them would have even bigger problems.

If they didn't stop Hitler, what else would the whole world have to face in the New Year?

Maybe something about Christmas gave the Allies new courage.

Or maybe they were just sick of being tied down in the snow.

But the day after Christmas, Patton broke through German forces around Bastogne. He and his army linked up with the 101st Airborne Division.

The Allies were on the offensive again, pushing the German army back.

And before New Year's Eve, the Ghost Army was called into action.

They covered an infantry unit as it moved up to the front, using a whole host of "special effects": fake road signs, unit insignia, and the old water point trick.

The freezing cold of the winter posed a whole new challenge.

"I thought it was hard to get one of these things inflated in the rain," someone complained. "Then I saw how bad they behave in winter. Both these armies might freeze to death before this thing blows up."

"It'll work," another soldier told him. "It just takes longer."

"A *lot* longer," his buddy added.

"Great," the first one said. "We'll just have the signal company radio over and let the Germans know we'll be ready for them sometime in June."

And it wasn't just the inflatables that didn't work in the cold.

Neither did their paint.

"This paint's made of oil," one of the men complained, squashing a clumped-up brush to the stencil he was using to change the markings on a jeep. "It shouldn't be freezing."

"Everything freezes when it gets cold enough," another soldier pointed out.

"Take your time," their commanding officer said. "Don't think of it as regular paint. Think of it as a new medium you're trying out."

"Yeah, ice paint," one of the soldiers said sarcastically.

"Hey, that sounds pretty good," the other one said. "Maybe it'll be the title of my first show, once we get out of all this."

Despite the new challenges of winter, their deception worked.

And once the infantry unit had safely moved up into the line, Patton wanted to remove a veteran unit for some rest and bring a fresh one up.

But the fresh unit was delayed.

So the Ghost Army was sent in to impersonate the veteran unit until the new one showed up.

Vic and his company played the parts of a field artillery battalion. They stenciled insignia on their helmets. They sewed on a new set of division patches. They put on the combat scarves the men of the unit wore.

They even displayed captured German souvenirs on their trucks, to make it look like they were a hardened combat unit that had captured German helmets and flags in the heat of battle.

And then when the fresh unit slipped safely into place,

the **Gh°st Army** faded away as if they had never **been there.**

Through the heart of that winter, the Ghost Army staged deceptions every few days.

Their base camp now was at Briey, in another gloomy French military barracks.

From there, they traveled all over France to protect Allied forces and confuse the Germans as Patton moved his forces into place.

But in the attic above their quarters at Briey, the Ghost Army set up an unusual source of R & R: a gallery.

In the quiet moments, the men still found time to paint and draw.

Keith Williams, another member of Vic's camouflage outfit, was even known to do watercolors while he was on guard duty. He used a brush made out of a few tiny hairs and three buttons of watercolor stuck on his watch.

In the gallery, the men took turns hanging their creations—and enjoying each other's work.

Somehow, stepping into the gallery felt like stepping into another place—a place far beyond the war.

Perhaps, when they stepped into the gallery, it gave

them a glimpse of what they were fighting for.

All the while, the Allies continued their offensive. Slowly but surely, they pushed the Germans out of France, back across the Rhine River into Germany.

In early March, Americans captured a bridge on the Rhine and sent a handful of forces across, into the German heartland.

But everyone knew this was only the first step.

To win the war, the Allies would need to win a decisive victory in Germany—on the other side of the Rhine.

(((•·~wwwwwwwwwwwwww·~wwww (((•))) ·wwww~wwwwwwwwww~•)))

In the dead of night, Vic and his unit worked overtime setting up dummy tanks. Around them, through the darkness, the sonic team broadcast the sounds of phantom men and machines moving into position.

The goal: to pretend they were an infantry division preparing for battle outside the German town of Saarlautern.

That would give the real infantry division time to get into place for the real attack they were planning farther north.

They'd done it all so many times before that they could practically work with their eyes closed.

But this operation
was
DIFFERENT.

They were working incredibly close to the German front lines.

So close that a German who took a good look at one of their inflatables might even be able to tell it wasn't real.

And in that case, the Ghost Army would be totally defenseless.

So Vic and his company were relieved the next day when they got word that the operation was finished.

They packed up their gear and piled into a truck, ready to move out.

Vic was sitting in the front of the truck, next to the driver, when the first shell hit.

The ground in front of them bucked and shook. It felt like an earthquake.

The next shell flew over their heads. It hit the truck in back of them. Metal sang and hissed through the air.

As Vic's ears rang, his mind raced.

Do I just tell them to get out of here now? he wondered.

Should he make a call on his own?

Should he wait for orders?

Just then, the radio crackled to life with the signal they'd been waiting for.

It was time to move.

No one had to tell them twice.

But not everybody was as lucky.

Another member of the Ghost Army, a sergeant just like Vic, was killed when his truck was hit by shrapnel. A captain died when his jeep was shelled.

Fifteen other men were wounded.

Some of them lost limbs.

They were the worst casualties the Ghost Army had suffered since the deception unit was formed.

And the big crossing into Germany, where everyone knew they'd face fierce German resistance, was still to come.

Just days after the artillery attack, the Ghost Army learned what part they'd play in the Rhine crossing.

A big one, it turned out.

General Dwight D. Eisenhower, then the Allies' top American commander, had planned to attack across the river on March 24.

One whole wing of his attack would be led by the American Ninth Army.

But Eisenhower wanted the Ghost Army to move into place on the banks of the Rhine a week *before* the real attack.

He wanted them to move up to face the German front lines, on their own, before any of the other Allied forces got there.

Their job: to convince the Germans that the Allied attack was going to come ten miles south of where Eisenhower had really planned it.

If the Germans didn't know where the attack was really coming from, they wouldn't be able to defend themselves.

And if the Germans didn't mount a tough defense, thousands of Allied lives would be saved.

But to complete the assignment, the Ghost Army would need to put on

the BIGGEST
deception

they'd ever attempted.

They weren't just pretending to be one unit this time. Or even one division.

They were pretending to be two separate divisions of the Ninth Army: the Thirtieth and the Seventy-Ninth. Those two divisions together included thirty thousand men.

There were just over a thousand in the Ghost Army.

To pull off this deception, every man in the Ghost Army would have to give the impression that there were thirty more of him, all poised to attack.

And they'd have to do it on the front lines, just across the river from the whole force of the German army. Who would be paying very close attention to everything the Ghost Army did as they waited for the Allied invasion that both sides knew might finally end the war.

Everything had to be perfect.

And that included perfect cooperation with the real divisions the Ghost Army was imitating.

As the real divisions pulled out, heading north to where Eisenhower was massing troops for the real attack, their radio operators all went silent. They'd planned the moment in advance with the radio operators of the Ghost Army.

At just that moment, Ghost Army radio operators began to broadcast.

They sounded just like the departing troops.

Except that the broadcasts by the Ghost Army made it sound as if those troops were moving south, not north.

To do this, the Ghost Army radio operators had to be on the move themselves.

One Ghost Army broadcaster transmitted thirty messages from eight different locations that first day to give the illusion that he was part of a division moving into the front line.

No **detail** was

too small

to notice.

Ghost Army radio operators even made sure they were broadcasting with the same amount of power as the radios they were replacing. They'd hold a pencil to the antennae of the real division radio to see how big a spark it made. Then they'd turn the dials on their own radio set until it made the same size spark.

In the meantime, Vic's camouflage unit was hard at work.

Near the town of Krefeld, on the Rhine, they set off smoke screen after smoke screen, sending giant clouds billowing across the fields.

Real army units sometimes set off smoke screens to make it harder for the Germans to see their numbers and equipment. But for the Ghost Army, smoke screens were a great deception tool. Because the Germans had gotten used to the idea that there were usually soldiers hiding behind the smoke, the Ghost Army could make the Germans believe there were thousands and thousands of soldiers moving in, when in fact there was literally nothing there but smoke.

They created phony supply dumps, stacks and stacks of empty boxes and barrels that didn't really contain any supplies.

They set up fake headquarters and filled them with soldiers dressed up as commanding officers.

Because the Luftwaffe had been so damaged in the previous years of the war, the Ghost Army hadn't dealt with much air surveillance before.

But now, in the final days of the war, the Germans threw everything they still had at the Allies.

Surveillance planes passed overhead constantly.

So Vic and his company were putting on a show this time not just for civilians on the ground but for spies overhead.

The camouflage company inflated pretty much every decoy tank and vehicle they had. They set them up in the forest, in the fields, and in the courtyards of buildings. When they were finished, two hundred inflatable vehicles were scattered around two small towns just west of the Rhine, more than they'd ever set up before.

Not only that, but the Allied command had ordered real tanks and guns to join the Ghost Army to help fool the Germans.

One real tank would be parked just outside a forest,

with the dummy tanks hidden just under the trees, where it was harder to tell they weren't real.

When the Ghost Army was given a few real antiaircraft guns, they beefed them up with eighty more dummy guns.

It looked like they were preparing for a huge battle.

They even set up two fake airfields, with inflatable observation planes on the fake runways.

By night, the sonic company broadcast the sounds of trucks rolling in to prepare for battle. By day, they played the sounds of pontoon bridges being built across the river: hammered metal, shouted orders, splashing water.

A real bridging unit even joined the Ghost Army and started to build an actual bridge across the Rhine to support the deception.

But all the fake tanks and bridges in the world wouldn't fool the enemy if there were no soldiers camped nearby.

So real infantry divisions joined the Ghost Army, too. They camped all around the phony attack site, drove their trucks through town, and pretended to man the phony tanks and guns.

The Ninth Army supported the Ghost Army with real firepower, too.

To make it look like the dummy guns were real, the Ninth Army increased their artillery fire from the area, to give the Germans the idea that this was just a little taste of the coming attack.

Ninth Army reconnaissance planes flew mission after mission over the fake attack zone, to give the impression that they were gathering intelligence for the big battle.

The Ninth Army even set up field hospitals around the positions the Ghost Army had taken, to make it look like they were preparing to deal with the casualties of the coming fight.

The people in the riverside towns the Ghost Army had camped around were clearly convinced.

Wherever Vic and his men went, they saw white flags on every door: a sign that people hoped would save their homes from destruction—or maybe even their lives.

And the Ghost Army managed to fool at least one pilot on their own side. In the days leading up to the invasion, an Allied plane landed on one of the Ghost Army's fake runways, thinking it was the real thing.

But the local people, and the confused pilot, weren't the Ghost Army's real audience.

They were performing this whole show for the Germans across the Rhine.

Had it
WORKED?

Did the Germans believe what they were seeing?

Were they over there on the other side of the river preparing for battle, too?

Or would they put up a deadly resistance ten miles north, where the real force of the Ninth Army was preparing their sneak attack?

There was **only** **ONE** **WAY** to find **out.**

The night before the Allied invasion, Allied leaders gathered near the river.

Early the next morning, the order went out: It was time to cross the Rhine.

On the banks, the soldiers steeled themselves for fierce combat.

They hoped this would be the last battle of the war, but no one expected it to come easy.

If the Allies had learned anything about the Germans during this war, it was that they wouldn't give up without a tough fight.

One by one, group by group, Allied soldiers began to cross the Rhine.

They marched across pontoon bridges.

They stood on the decks of navy landing craft.

They held their breath and scanned the opposite banks.

Every single one of them was waiting for the fierce blast of German opposition they expected to rain down on them: bursting shells and screaming bullets that would leave wounds and steal lives and blow their bridges and ships to pieces.

But **nothing happened.**

(((•~wwwwwwwwww~wwww~(((•)))~wwww~wwwwwwwww~•)))

When the Ninth Army got to the other side of the Rhine, the few Germans they found there seemed surprised—as if they were expecting the attack to come somewhere else.

The Allies had expected fierce German fighters.

They found feeble, disorganized troops.

Thousands of Allied soldiers streamed into Germany that day.

Allied leaders had feared they might suffer as many as ten thousand casualties in the crossing.

Instead, fewer than fifty lives were lost.

The final crossing into Germany, for the invasion that

ended the war, had cost fewer lives than some training exercises.

And in the battle that followed, the Allies learned one reason why.

Captured German documents let Allied leaders see what plans the Germans had made in the days before the invasion.

And those documents showed that the Germans believed the bulk of the Ninth Army was ten miles south of the real crossing—right where the Ghost Army's deception put them.

((•-ᴡᴡᴡᴡᴡᴡᴡ-((•))-ᴡᴡᴡᴡᴡᴡᴡ-•))

With the crossing of the Rhine, the war in Europe was soon over.

Allied forces raced across Germany so quickly that there was no more call for deception.

So the Ghost Army was assigned to guard camps full of people who had been forced from their homes by the war.

There were thousands of them from dozens of countries.

Vic and his buddies couldn't wait to get home. But these people didn't even know if they still had homes to go back to.

So while they were all waiting, Vic began to sketch.

He asked one person to sit for him, and the next thing he knew, three or four more were waiting to have their pictures drawn, too.

Proud young men. Tired old men. Worried old women. Young women in beautiful costumes. Sometimes Vic would sketch dozens of them in a single day.

His buddies sketched, too.

When each portrait was done, they'd have the people sign their names to them: a symbol that,

no matter

what **had happened**

to them in the war,

they **had** **made** **it** **through.**

These were the faces of the people the Ghost Army had been fighting for.

And they were the people who would build the new world together, now that the war was over.

Can you decipher
Vic's letter to find
out where he left his
sketchbook behind?

G K NGWFT,
MUR   Z I'

Q   EV   OD   H   LQW   M   BE SO YFTA
NI O Y SI SOV   PK UI   BYDZANAPT

 D H KG   LBT   KSZ   J   JN M ZG
GI NOX   PHY   N QLCH MS WGIGLBZFYL.

SV'   DYVR   PE   J B   TLU PM FHX
ZL'J CO EX GD   ZIV   C DB KU   Y

D VJ F   B OYQ   YULH LB   OK PFT
UV XID HT SUF   Q EQBGBFS DC   C

 O XO - M   WRO NY.   FO   U   NLRMZ
UXPBHV-ATG BB VKU   TUY DRE X AU

R   C   S   HE D   D   XU   T KX
AP EY VR WOXJ AIU   RWI ZRY   ?

HUA
XXX

Historical Note

The members of the Ghost Army were chosen because they were all great at telling stories: with sound, paint, or drama.

But they were also good at keeping a secret.

And because the Ghost Army wasn't declassified until 1996, many of them kept the secret of their exploits during the war for most of their lives.

Once the secret was out, though, an amazing story unfolded—both in declassified government documents and in the recollections, stories, and sketches of the men of the Ghost Army.

So all the details in this story are true. The Ghost Army really went to all the places they go in this book, and they really pulled off all the deceptions in this story. Even the thoughts and feelings of Victor and his fellow artists and soldiers are based in fact, drawn from their interviews, writings, and letters.

Victor didn't win the war alone. He represents all the men who risked their lives as part of the Ghost Army.

None of them could have done it on their own. But together they accomplished something that even the greatest artist might not have been able to imagine.